NATIONAL GEOGRAPHIC

Fruit Salad

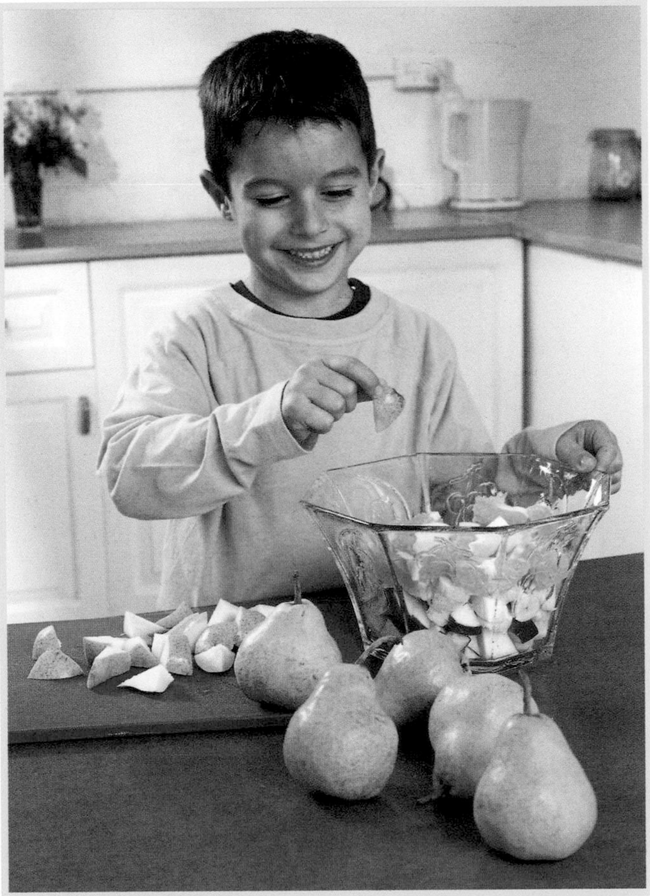

Ming Tan

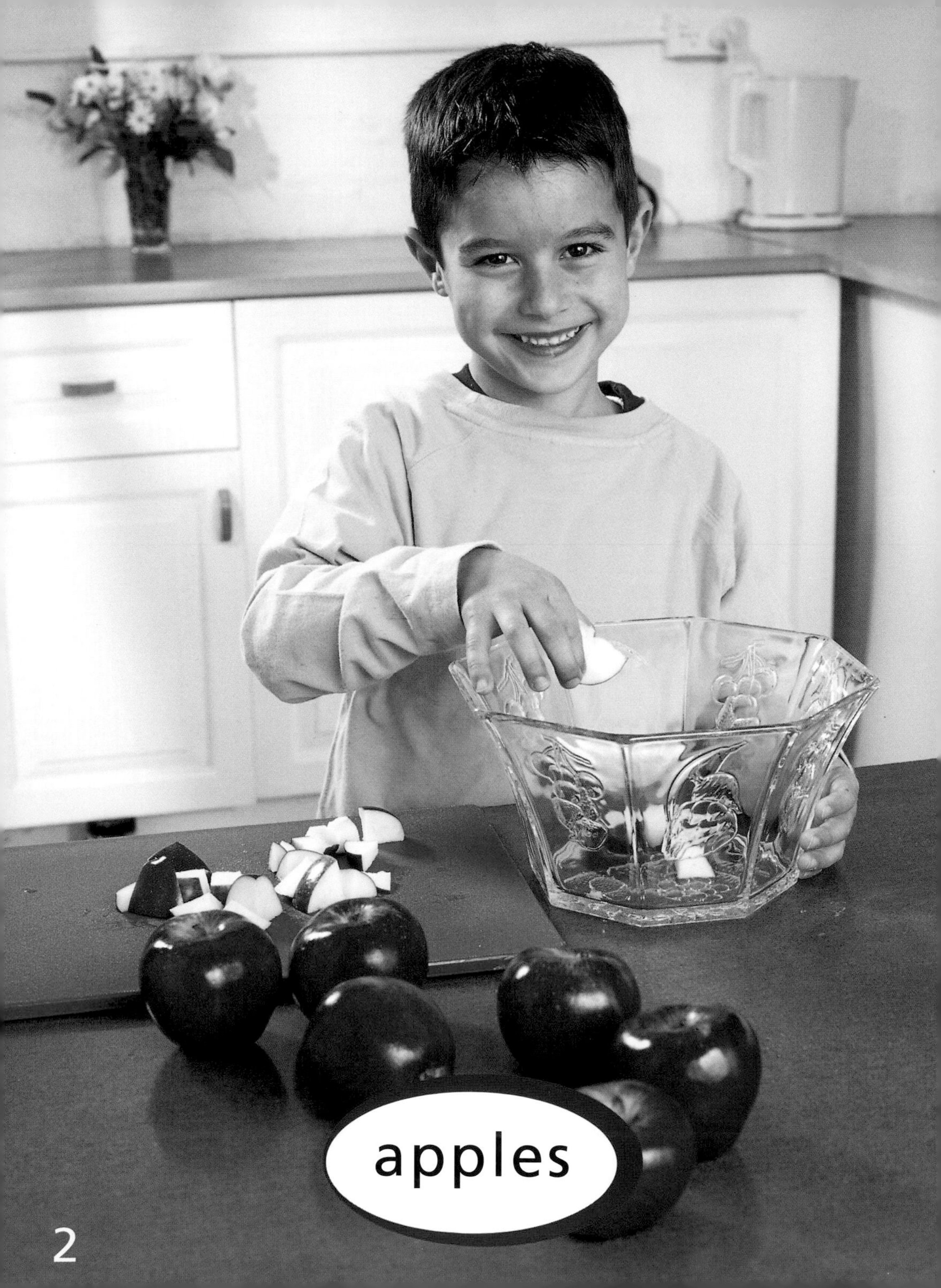

apples

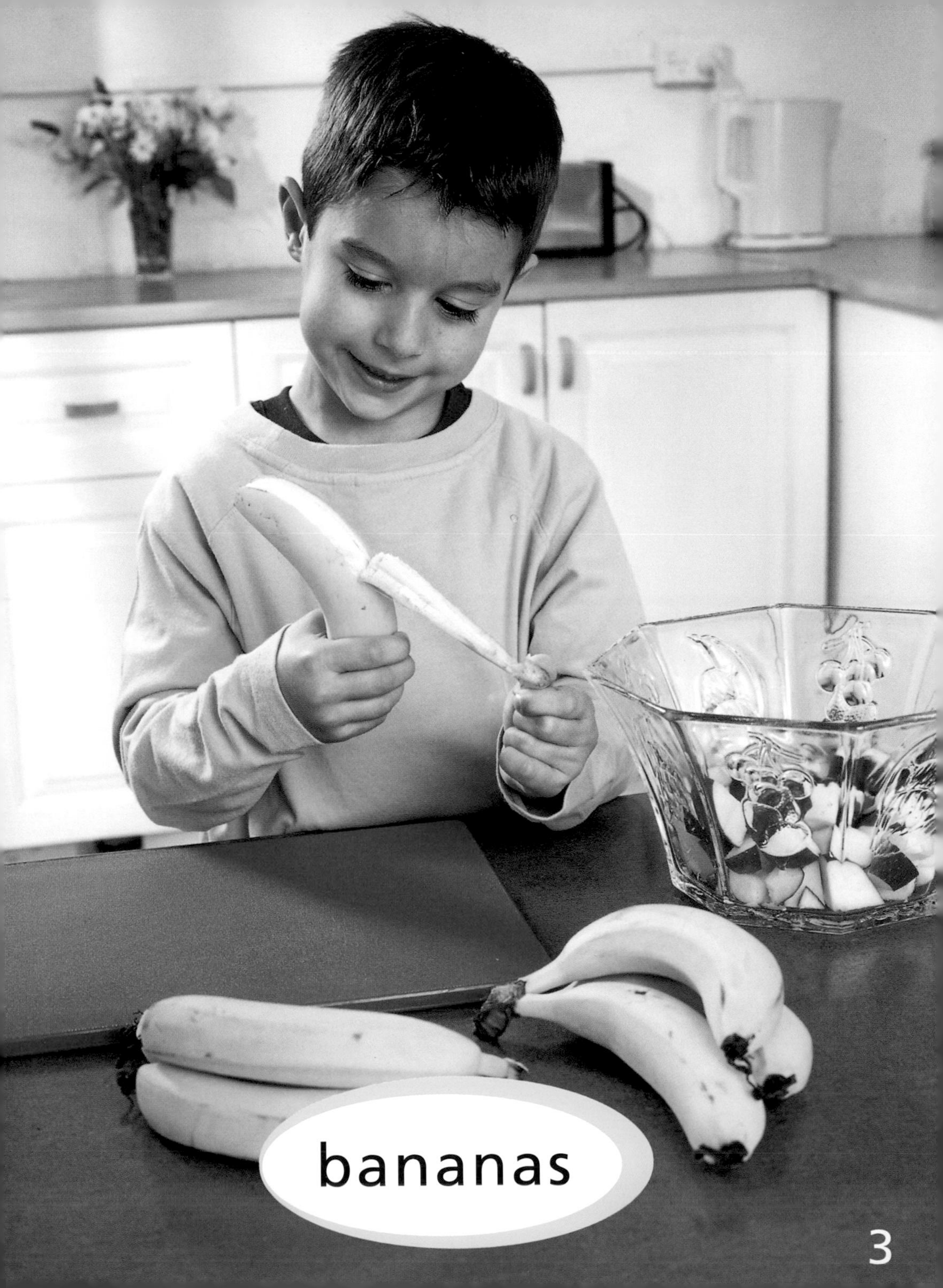

bananas

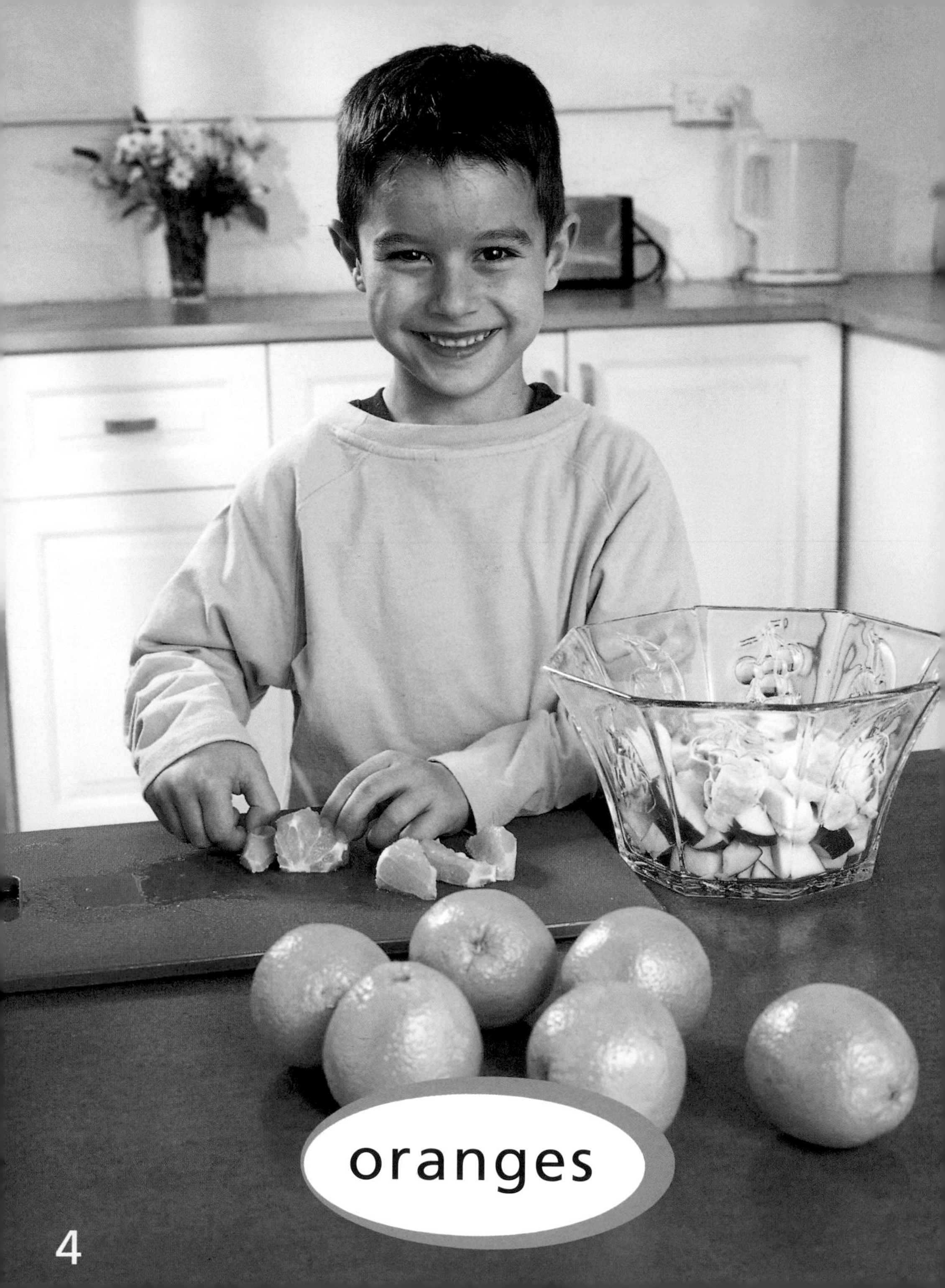
oranges

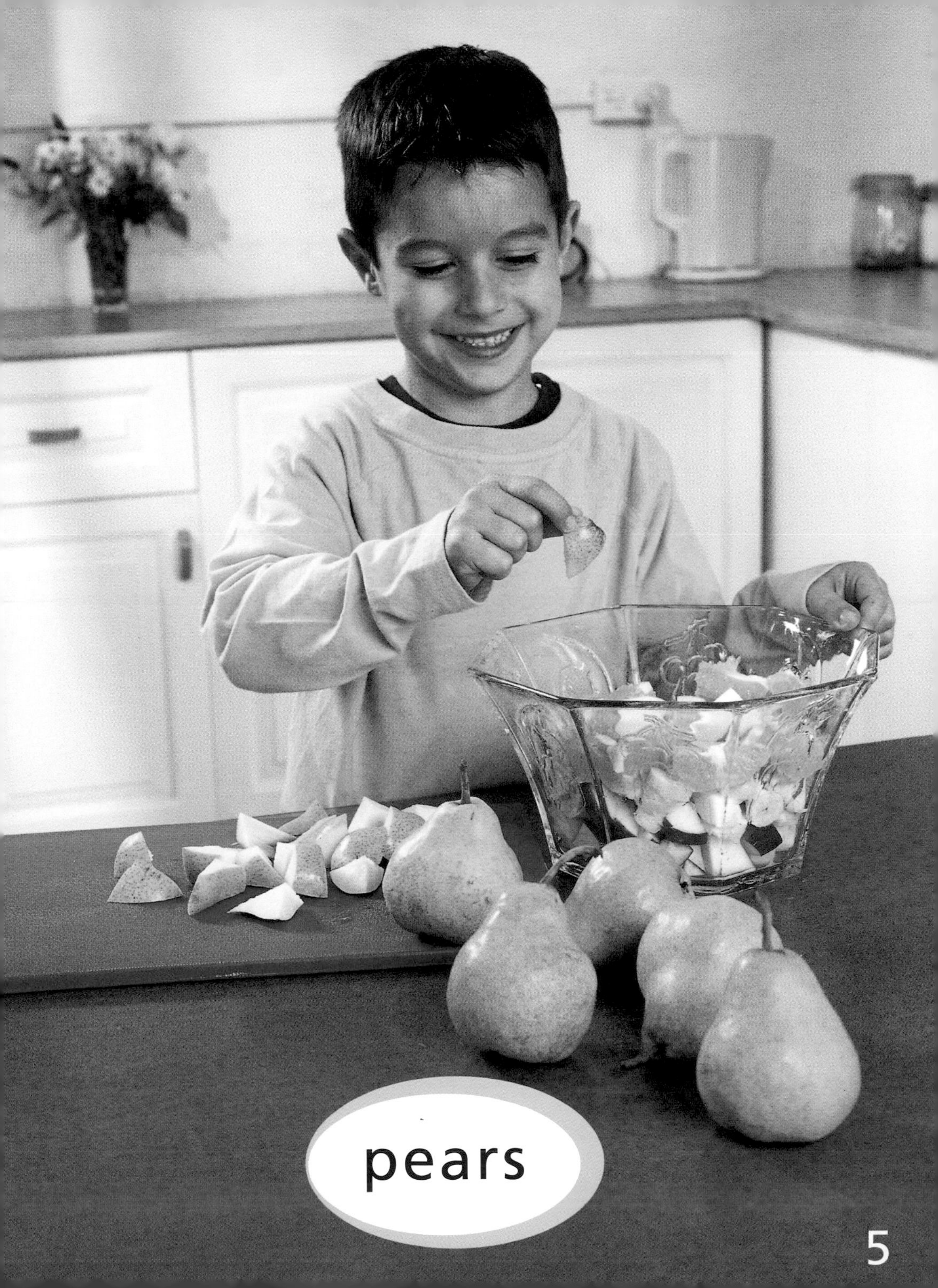

pears

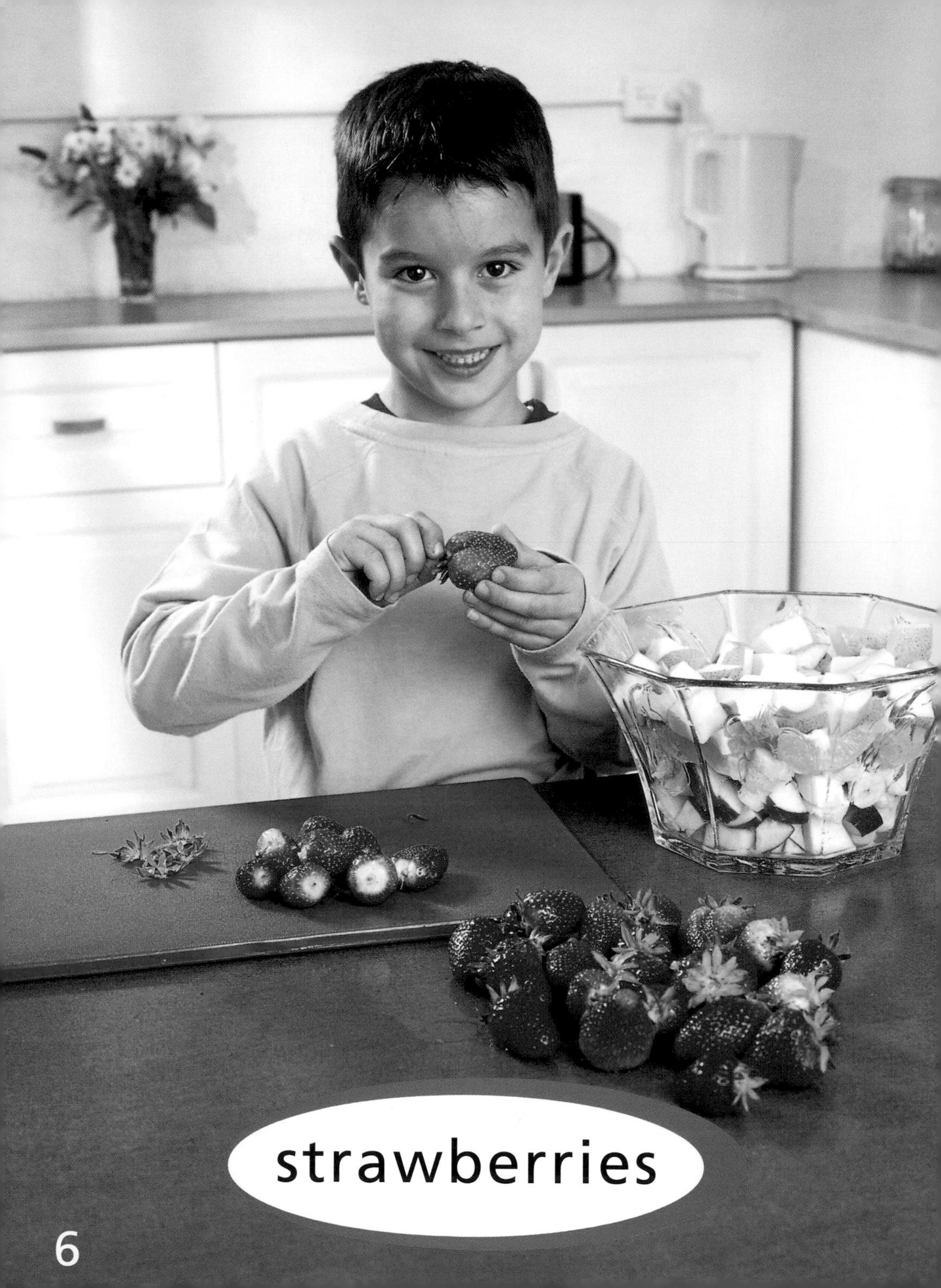

strawberries

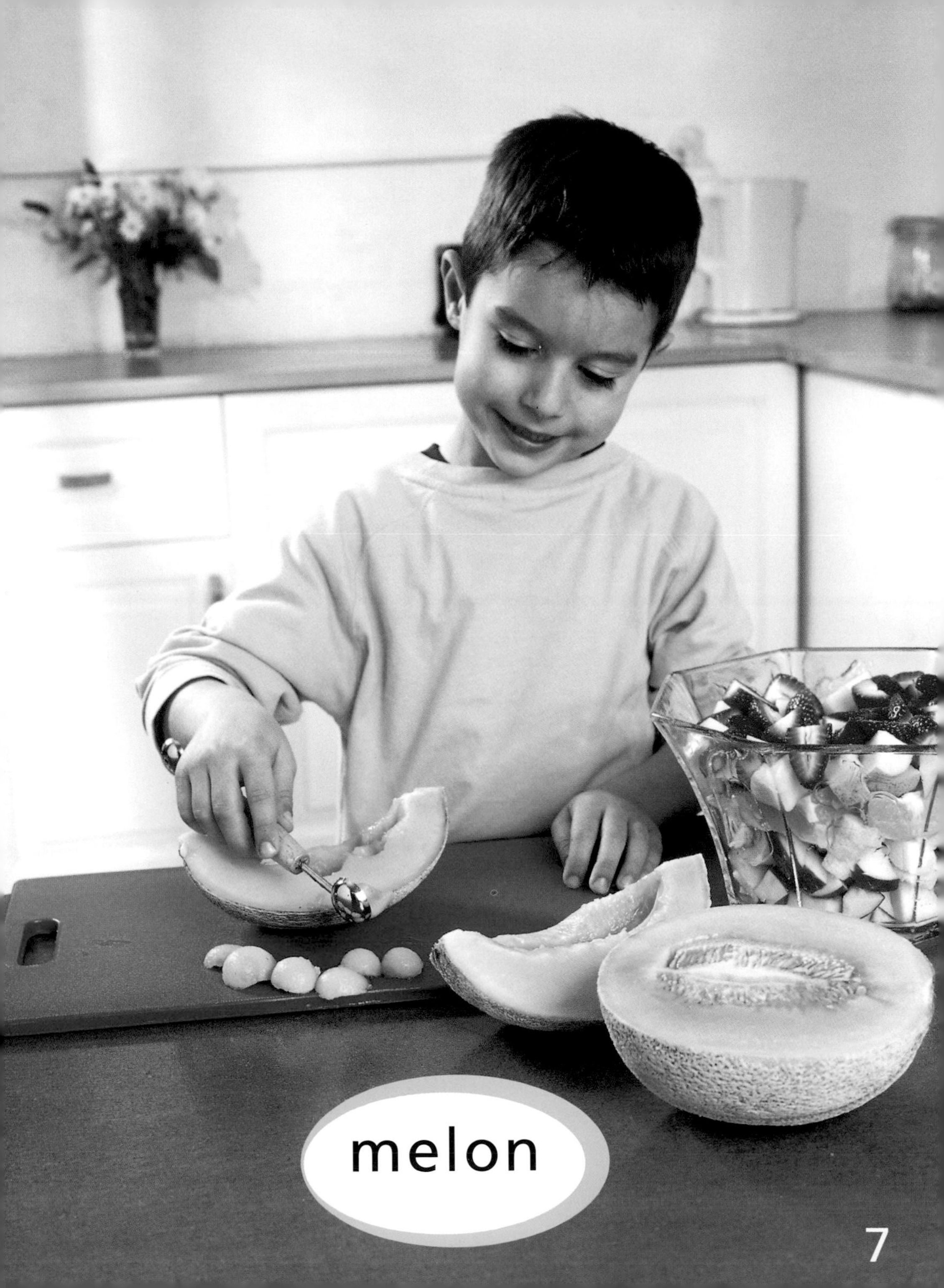

melon

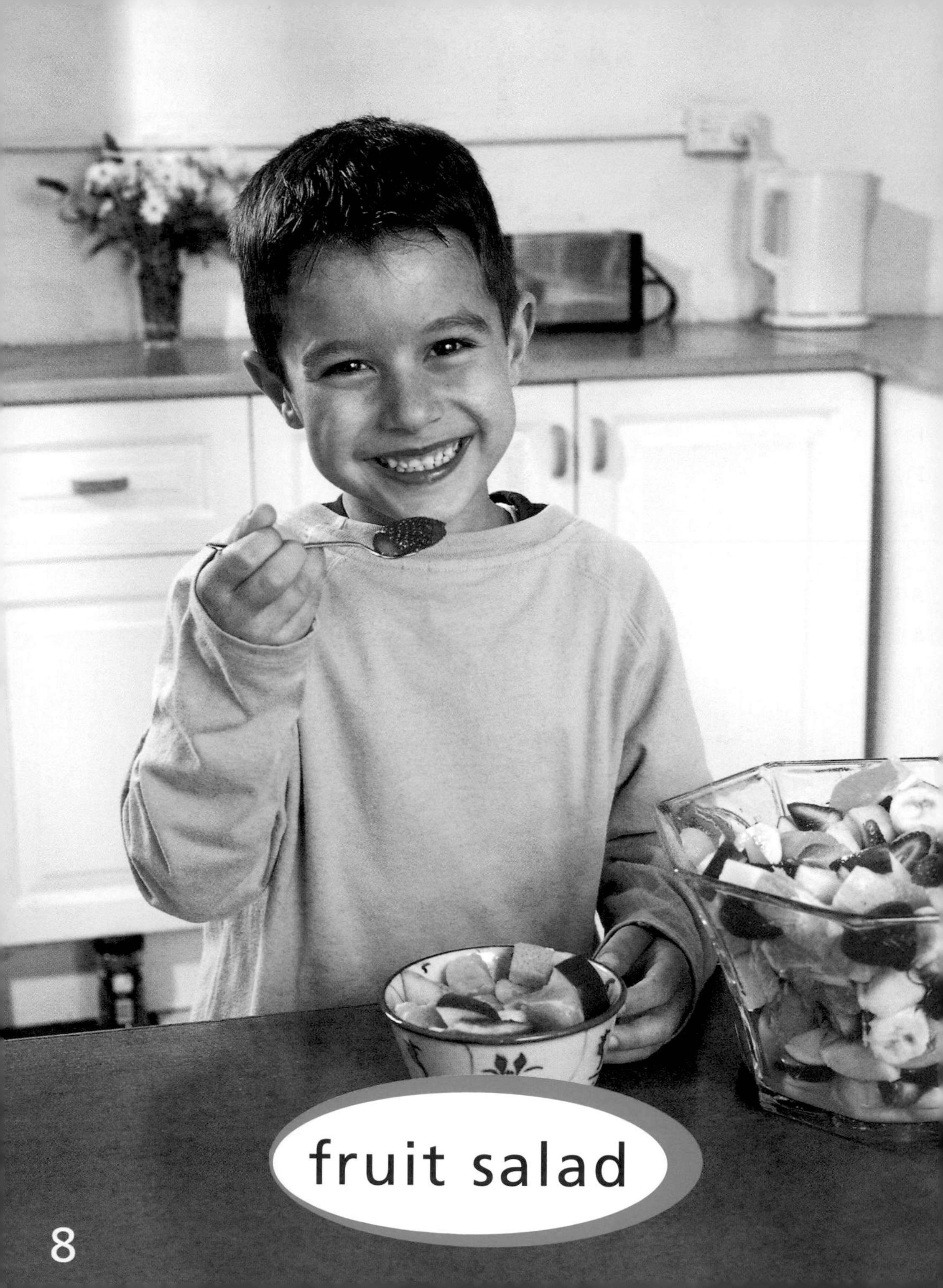

fruit salad